SPOTLIGHT ON NATIVE AMERICANS

INUIT

Jayson Chesterfield

PowerKiDS press™

New York

Published in 2016 by The Rosen Publishing Group, Inc.
29 East 21st Street, New York, NY 10010

First Edition

Editor: Karolena Bielecki
Book Design: Kris Everson
Reviewed by: Robert J. Conley, Former Sequoyah Distinguished Professor at Western Carolina University and Director of Native American Studies at Morningside College and Montana State University
Supplemental material reviewed by: Donald A. Grinde, Jr., Professor of Transnational/American Studies at the State University of New York at Buffalo.

Photo credits: Cover © iStockphoto.com/IPGGutenbergUKLtd; pp. 4–5 Wayne Lynch/All Canada Photos/Getty Images; pp. 7, 12, 15, 20, 23, 27 Corbis; pp. 9, 11 (left) Peter Newark's American Pictures; pp. 11 (right), 18 (inset) Native Stock; p. 14 Yvette Cardozo/Photolibrary/Getty Images, pp. 16–17 Michelle Valberg/ All Canada Photos/Getty Images, pp. 18–19 Frank Olsen/Moment Open/ Getty Images; p. 25 Richard Oisenius/National Geographic/Getty Images; p. 29 Tom Hanson/AFP/Getty Images.

Library of Congress Cataloging-in-Publication Data

Chesterfield, Jayson.
  Inuit / Jayson Chesterfield.
      pages cm. — (Spotlight on Native Americans)
  Includes bibliographical references and index.
  ISBN 978-1-4994-1671-8 (pbk.)
  ISBN 978-1-4994-1670-1 (6 pack)
  ISBN 978-1-4994-1673-2 (library binding)
  1. Inuit—History—Juvenile literature. 2. Inuit—Social life and customs—Juvenile literature. I. Title.
  E99.E7C5315 2015
  305.897'12—dc23
                                                    2015007811

Manufactured in the United States of America

CPSIA Compliance Information: Batch #WS15PK: For Further Information contact Rosen Publishing, New York, New York at 1-800-237-9932

CONTENTS

The Inuit Homelands. 4

People of the Arctic Tundra. 6

The Age of Exploration. 8

European Influence. .10

Inuit People in the Twentieth Century. 12

Surviving in the Arctic. 14

Inuit Society. 16

Inuit Beliefs.. 18

Old Customs and Modern Life. 20

Inuit Work and Art. 22

Problems Facing the Inuit Today. 24

Fighting for Inuit Rights 26

Nunavut: "Our Land". 28

Glossary 30

For More Information 31

Index. 32

THE INUIT HOMELANDS
CHAPTER 1

The Inuit are a people who inhabit **Arctic** and **subarctic** regions. Their homelands in North America include northern parts of Canada, Alaska, and the eastern and western coasts of Greenland. A small number of Inuits also live in Siberia. The total Inuit population today is about 155,000.

Some Inuit groups go by different names. The Native American people of Arctic Canada and West Greenland call themselves *Inuit*. Other names are *Inupiat*, *Yupik*, and *Inuvialut*. All these names mean "people" or "real people." In 1977, representatives from the various Inuit groups met in Alaska and decided they would use *Inuit* to describe all the different groups.

Scientists believe that the Inuits came from Asia long ago. However, most of the Inuit groups tell their own origin story. In the distant past, a young girl was forced to

The Arctic **tundra** is similar to a desert because it receives little rainfall each year and few plants can grow there. Just 400 people live year-round on Canada's Ellesmere Island, shown here.

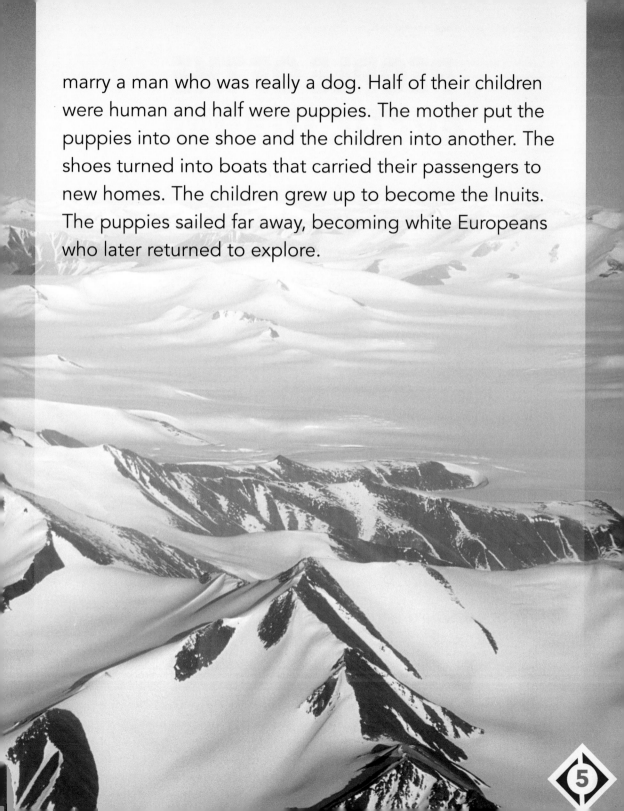

marry a man who was really a dog. Half of their children were human and half were puppies. The mother put the puppies into one shoe and the children into another. The shoes turned into boats that carried their passengers to new homes. The children grew up to become the Inuits. The puppies sailed far away, becoming white Europeans who later returned to explore.

PEOPLE OF THE ARCTIC TUNDRA

CHAPTER 2

The first people to live in the Arctic tundra of North America are sometimes called Paleoeskimos. *Paleo* means "ancient," and *Eskimo* was the name European explorers gave the Inuits. The name came from an Algonquian Indian word referring to snowshoes—not to eating raw meat, as some people once thought.

The Paleoeskimos included the Dorset and Thule (TOO-lee) peoples. The Dorsets first appeared in northern Alaska about 5,000 years ago. They then moved eastward into Canada and Greenland, living along the coast.

About 1,200 years ago, a new **culture** developed in Alaska, known today as the Thule people. The Thules were skillful sailors and hunters who followed the Dorsets eastward across North America, sailing through the many islands of northern Canada.

About A.D. 900, the temperature in the Arctic began to rise slowly. As the ice in Arctic waters began to melt, whales began moving eastward, and the Thules

Siberian Inuits in traditional **parkas** perform a dance. Inuit dances sometimes act out folktales or copy the movement of animals.

followed, because the whales provided most of the Thules' food. No one knows why the Dorsets fled or died off as the Thules took over their lands. The Thules were the **ancestors** of today's Inuits in North America; their languages and culture come from the Thules.

THE AGE OF EXPLORATION
CHAPTER 3

Starting in the fifteenth century, several European nations sent ships to explore the world. In the late sixteenth century, European sea captains thought they could sail through the Arctic Ocean and reach China. They called this supposed shortcut to Asia the Northwest Passage; their search for it led to the first contact between Europeans and the Inuits of Canada.

In 1576, English explorer Martin Frobisher reached Baffin Island in northern Canada while looking for the Northwest Passage. He met some Inuits and took one back with him to England. Frobisher returned the next year, but the cold conditions made it too difficult for his settlers to colonize. During Frobisher's second voyage, in 1577, the English battled the Inuits. After his men killed several Inuits, Frobisher took two more Inuits—a woman and her child—and returned home with his captives. In England, the Inuit man demonstrated how he hunted with a spear and paddled his **kayak**. He and the other two Inuits died within a month of reaching England, probably from **pneumonia**.

Over the next century, other Europeans continued to sail into Canada's Arctic region, looking for the Northwest Passage. Like Frobisher, they had limited contact with the Inuits.

In this seventeenth-century painting, European explorers and Canadian Inuits battle. Few Europeans reached the center of the Canadian Arctic until the nineteenth century.

EUROPEAN INFLUENCE

CHAPTER 4

In general, the Europeans lacked the Inuits' skills for surviving in the harsh Arctic climate. Through their trading posts and whaling ports, however, Europeans influenced how the Inuits lived. More Inuits focused on the fur trade. With more frequent contact, the Inuits began to rely more on European goods and less on traditional tools and ways of life.

The arrival of the Europeans also led to problems among the Inuits. During the nineteenth century, European diseases spread among the Inuits for the first time, killing many of them. Other Inuits developed **alcoholism** after the Europeans began trading them alcohol for their furs. Whalers killed so many whales that their numbers fell, threatening a key Inuit food source.

The Europeans also tried to change the Inuits' traditional religious beliefs. In Alaska, **missionaries** from the Russian Orthodox Church taught the Inuits the Christian religion. Protestant missionaries from England did the same in parts of Canada. Some Inuits accepted

(Left) These hunters would have eaten almost every part of the seal they just killed. The Inuits ate seal meat raw, boiled, frozen, and dried. *(Right)* Today, some Inuits in Alaska still go to Russian Orthodox churches.

the Europeans' faith. Others became Christian while still following some of their old religious traditions. The missionaries provided medical care for the Inuits and taught them European languages.

INUIT PEOPLE IN THE TWENTIETH CENTURY

CHAPTER 5

During the twentieth century, Canada, the United States, and Denmark controlled the Arctic lands of North America. The governments of these countries promoted education and assimilation—the process of forcing the Inuits to accept U.S. and European culture.

This Inuit village on Little Diomede Island, Alaska, was once a spring hunting site, but residents now live there year-round. In the local language, the village is called Inalik.

In the past, most Inuits **migrated** between summer and winter hunting or fishing grounds. Under Western influence, they began to settle in permanent communities. By the 1960s and 1970s, more Inuits had indoor plumbing and electricity. Some Inuits began working at Canadian and U.S. companies. In Alaska, the discovery of oil and the growth of the salmon fishing industry created jobs.

In 1924, the Inuits of Alaska became U.S. citizens. In 1959, Alaska became the forty-ninth state. Inuits and other Alaskans could now elect political representatives.

By that time, most Canadian Inuits lived in a region known as the Northwest Territories, where only some were represented in Parliament, which is Canada's lawmaking body. After 1962, the entire region elected a representative to Parliament. They now had more control over lawmaking. Inuits across Canada also played a larger role in running their own affairs. Starting in 1953, the Inuits of Greenland also won more freedom from the Danish government to control politics in their homeland.

SURVIVING IN THE ARCTIC
CHAPTER 6

During the winter, temperatures in some parts of the Arctic can drop below -40° Fahrenheit (-40° Celsius). The Sun provides almost no light for months at a time. Farming is impossible, so the Inuits became experts at hunting and fishing. In the brief, warmer Arctic summer, the Inuits could gather nuts, roots, and berries as well as hunt and fish.

During a typical year, most Inuits migrated from one area to another, searching for food. The Copper Inuits of central Canada, for example, hunted seals during the winter by searching for air holes in the ice. Hunters waited for the seals at the holes, then speared them with

This photo from the early twentieth century shows Alaskan Inuit hunters in their umiak. Modern umiaks use motors for power instead of sails and oars.

harpoons. During the summer, the Copper Inuits moved onto land and fished or hunted caribou, musk ox, and other animals.

In other regions, such as Alaska, the Inuits sailed on small boats called umiaks to hunt for large sea mammals, such as walrus and whale, in the spring. Inuits across the Arctic also hunted in kayaks. Similar to canoes, these boats were built for just one person. Both boats were made of wood and covered with animal skins. In general, most of the whale and walrus hunters also killed bear, fox, rabbit, and duck.

INUIT SOCIETY

CHAPTER 7

The need to migrate meant the Inuits did not build large, permanent towns. Still, the Inuits usually had certain areas where they returned year after year. Several families would form groups called bands, and bands united to form small communities. The families within a band or community might be related, but often two fathers formed a friendship that united their families. A family or band might decide to leave a certain community after a year or two.

The Inuits did not have formal governments or politics. The men of a community usually made decisions by debating an issue and coming to an agreement. In some regions, an older or very wealthy man might have more influence.

When food was scarce, the communities made sure that everyone received something from a successful hunt. The sharing was most common after killing a large sea mammal, with the largest portions going to the hunters. If food was available, the Inuits would not let someone starve.

Ikpiarjuk, in Nunavut, Canada, was often occupied by nomadic Inuits. Today, hundreds of people live there permanently.

INUIT BELIEFS

CHAPTER 8

According to traditional Inuit beliefs, the world is filled with spirits. Across the Arctic, the Inuits had different names and ideas about these spirits. In general, the spirits were invisible beings that filled the world. Sometimes they were ghosts of dead people or animals. The Inuits believed these spirits caused most of the illnesses, accidents, and other bad events that trouble humans. The Inuits feared the spirits and did not like to discuss them.

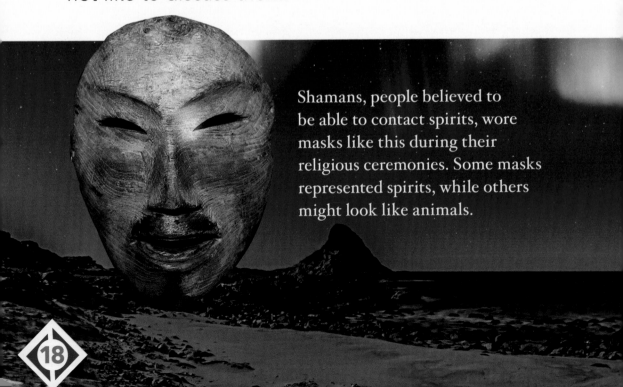

Shamans, people believed to be able to contact spirits, wore masks like this during their religious ceremonies. Some masks represented spirits, while others might look like animals.

The Inuits also believed that humans had **souls**. Many Inuits thought animals had souls too, and some said everything in the world, including plants and rocks, had souls. The entire universe had a breath-soul commonly called Sila, which was associated with the air and weather. While alive, a person had a breath-soul connected to Sila and a free-soul created by three goddesses—the Indweller in the Earth, the Sea Mother, and the Caribou Mother. Only the free-soul survived after a person died, usually traveling on to another world and then entering another human to live again.

In Arctic regions, the aurora borealis sometimes sets the night sky aglow. Traditional Inuit stories speak of these "Northern Lights" as the dancing spirits of ancestors or animals.

OLD CUSTOMS AND MODERN LIFE

CHAPTER 9

Today, most Inuits blend old customs with modern ways of life. They still hunt caribou and seal on the tundra. Instead of riding on dog sleds, however, they

Snowmobiles are expensive to buy and run, but they help the Inuits travel across the tundra. Many Inuits use them for hunting.

speed across the ice and snow on snowmobiles. Planes transport people and supplies. In Inuit towns, people drive **all-terrain vehicles**.

Small houses and log cabins have replaced the tents and **sod** homes. In some areas, the Inuits still build **igloos** while camping or hunting. Since sealskins dry out in heated homes, women in central Canada prefer to work with sealskins in snow houses nearby. The Inuits wear the animal skins and furs along with modern clothing.

Most Inuit children go to public schools, and some go on to colleges and universities in larger cities to the south. Over the past few decades, the Inuits have fought to make sure their schools teach Inuit language and culture. They teach students how to prepare traditional foods and use animal hides for clothing. At the same time, the children need to learn about the outside world if they plan to leave their small Arctic communities. Television, the Internet, and other media have helped the Inuits learn more about the world beyond the tundra.

INUIT WORK AND ART
CHAPTER 10

Many Inuits earn their income by traditional methods, such as trapping animals for their furs and fishing. Some Inuits work in the mining or oil industries. They also work in their communities as teachers, police officers, store clerks and managers, and government officials.

Some Inuits make their living in the arts. Inuit artists sculpt, paint, and make prints, often showing scenes of Arctic life. Many mix modern techniques with traditional Inuit art forms. World famous for his work in stone, **ivory**, and other materials, Osuitok Ipeelee (1922–2005) of Nunavut, the Inuits' modern homeland in Canada, began carving in the 1940s. His subjects included traditional Inuit images such as birds, seals, and caribou. Another well-known carver is Oviloo Tunnillie (1949–2014), a Nunavut Inuit best known for her female figures. Her father Toonoo was one of the first successful Inuit sculptors.

Inuit writers, working in both Native and European languages, are reporters and novelists. Some write

An Inuit artist prepares to make a print. Some Inuit printmakers in Cape Dorset, Canada, cut an image into stone, apply ink to the image, and then make their prints.

down ancient Inuit folktales, while others examine how the Inuits live in the modern world. Mitiarjuk Attasie Nappaaluk (1931–2007) wrote *Sanaaq*, the first novel in the Inuktitut language. Her story looks at Inuit life from a female point of view.

PROBLEMS FACING THE INUIT TODAY

CHAPTER 11

Over the last few decades, many Inuits have developed serious illnesses related to their lifestyles and their **environment**. **Obesity**, tooth decay, **diabetes**, heart disease, high blood pressure, and cancer are all much more common in Inuits than they were decades ago.

One of the reasons for this ill health is a change in the Inuit diet. Today the Inuits eat less fresh local meat and buy more high-calorie fast foods and beverages, which have very little nutritional value. The meat and fish the Inuits traditionally ate was good for their hearts, and the exercise of hunting and fishing also kept them healthy. As they exchanged a hunting lifestyle for less active jobs, many Inuits have developed diseases common in other parts of North America. They are also becoming shortsighted. Some experts think this may also be related to diet, while others believe it is caused by reading and computer use.

Another reason for Inuit ill health is that many Inuits smoke, drink too much alcohol, and take drugs. Many of them have found it difficult to adjust to a new way of living and have lost their sense of identity. This has led to depression and, in some cases, suicide.

These Inuit children are consuming unhealthy imported foods and beverages rather than traditional meats. The Inuits are now experiencing health problems similar to people in other parts of North America who also eat a lot of fast food.

FIGHTING FOR INUIT RIGHTS

CHAPTER 12

Over the last few decades, the Inuits have tried to make sure the governments that control their lands do not ignore them or take away their rights.

In the 1960s, the Inuits of Quebec, Canada, objected to business plans to use their land for mining, forestry, and **hydroelectricity** developments. They took their case to court, forcing the Quebec and Canadian governments to negotiate with them. This led in 1978 to an agreement in which the Inuit were paid **compensation**. They also gained limited self-government.

In 2002, the Alaskan Inuits convinced an international whaling organization to raise the limit on the number of bowhead whales they could kill. The next year, the Inuits of Greenland won a court case that required the Danish government to give them money for forcing them from their homes years before.

In 2014, Inuit living in Nunavut created a Facebook group to raise awareness over high food costs in the

A Nunavut mother and son stand near a stone sculpture called an *inuksuk*. An *inuksuk* can be thousands of years old and might mark a path or warn of dangerous conditions.

region. Many Inuit families face food insecurity because goods can easily cost twice as much (or more) than they do in less-remote parts of Canada. The Nunavut Food Security Coalition is trying to encourage Inuits to again rely on hunting as they did long ago as one solution.

NUNAVAT: "OUR LAND"
CHAPTER 13

In 1999, the Canadian government turned a large portion of the Northwest Territories into a homeland for the Inuits called Nunavut ("our land"). About 29,000 people, mostly Inuits, live in this huge territory, which covers about 772,200 square miles (2 million square kilometers), an area larger than Alaska.

Two Inuit languages are spoken in Nunavut as well as Canada's two official languages, English and French. The territory has just 26 communities, and the capital, Iqaluit, has a population of about 6,000. Towns are isolated, with no roads connecting them. The people must fly or sail to travel across the territory.

The creation of Nunavut gave the Inuits of the region local political control. The Nunavut government consists of elected members and a council of advisors who make sure traditional Inuit culture and knowledge are part of government decisions.

After Nunavut was created, the only Inuits in Canada without any self-government were those in the province of Labrador. Then, in 2005, the Government

Inuits celebrate the creation of Nunavut in 1999 by displaying the new Nunavut flag, which has an *inuksuk* in the center.

of Nunatsiavut ("our beautiful land") was created. Its elected members can make new laws about Inuit education, health, and culture.

Long ago, the Inuits developed skills and knowledge that made life possible in a harsh climate. Today, they keep their traditions alive.

GLOSSARY

alcoholism: A disease in which people's desire to drink alcohol is so strong they cannot control it.

all-terrain vehicle: A small, open, four-wheeled vehicle with large tires that can move easily over ice and snow.

ancestor: A person from whom an individual is descended.

Arctic: The cold regions south of the North Pole that reach as far as an imaginary line named the Arctic Circle.

compensation: Money given to people in return for a loss, such as a loss of Native American land.

culture: The arts, beliefs, and customs that form a people's way of life.

diabetes: A disease in which there is a lack of a sugar-controlling chemical named insulin in the human body.

environment: The natural world.

harpoon: A spear with a rope attached so the throwers can pull their catch toward them.

hydroelectricity: Electricity produced by water power.

igloo: A dome-shaped dwelling built of blocks of hardened snow.

ivory: The long tusk, or tooth, of certain mammals, such as a walrus.

kayak: A long, thin canoe usually built for one person.

migrate: To move from one area to another.

missionary: Someone who travels to teach others their religion.

obesity: A medical condition in which body fat has accumulated to the point of causing health problems.

parka: A warm fur jacket with a hood.

pneumonia: A serious illness that makes it difficult for a person to breathe.

sod: Grass or turf.

soul: Energy or an invisible force thought to create human life or be connected to gods. Also, the spiritual part of a human being.

subarctic: The cold region immediately south of the Arctic.

tundra: A cold region with few or no trees and a layer of soil beneath the surface that always stays frozen.

FOR MORE INFORMATION

BOOKS

Benoit, Peter, and Kevin Cunningham. *The Inuit.* New
  York, NY: Scholastic, Inc., 2011.

Manning, Jack. *Igloos.* North Mankato, MN: Capstone
  Press, 2014.

Young, Dan. *Life Among the Inuit.* New York, NY: Rosen
  Publishing Group, 2013.

WEBSITES

Due to the changing nature of Internet links, PowerKids Press has
developed an online list of websites related to the subject of this book.
This site is updated regularly. Please use this link to access the list:
www.powerkidslinks.com/sona/inui

INDEX

A
ancestor, 7, 19
Arctic, 4, 6, 8, 9, 10, 12, 14, 15, 18, 19, 21, 22
arts, 22, 23

B
bands, 16

C
culture, 6, 7, 12, 21, 28, 29

D
Dorsets, 6, 7,

E
Europeans, 5, 6, 8, 9, 10, 11, 12, 22

F
fur, 10, 21, 22

G
government, 12, 13, 17, 22, 26, 28

H
hunt, 6, 8, 11, 12, 13, 14, 15, 17, 20, 21, 24, 27

K
kayak, 8, 15

L
lifestyle, 24, 25

M
migrate, 13, 14, 16

N
Nunavut, 17, 22, 26, 27, 28, 29

R
religion, 10, 11, 18

S
seal, 11, 14, 20, 21, 22

T
Thule, 6, 7
traditional stories, 4, 19, 23
tundra, 4, 6, 20, 21

U
umiak, 15